Paper Moon

**A journey through words
to a place of love and healing.**

Natasha Tynan

For Jack and George, the guiding stars in my life.

Acknowledgements

Thank you to one of the most beautiful hearts in my life, my sister Laura, for inspiring courage to write and share this book. To my sister Karen for her unyielding love and support. To my husband, who has no idea about poetry but who consistently believes in me. To my parents for teaching me how the power of love can change your life forever.

Author's Note

Paper Moon opens up new pathway's for your mind and fills your soul with peace. It is written in ink from my veins and dotted with tears of love. It is a gift from my heart, and I hope you enjoy reading it.

-Natasha.

Introduction

Paper Moon

in the halo between stars and moon,
burning dust falls beneath darkness of
peaks, where glitters of fire, no longer
dancing inside my heart, lie
buried under ash and tears stained in
fear, drench the land,

a stream of thought,
glistening in crystal speckled froth,
fizzles on clandestine shores as step by
step, a cloud of memories imprint in
castles of time and I, wrapped in words
from chiselled glass, sail across the
storm of life,

but in shadows of dawn a rainbow
unveils, piercing the mist of silence,
illuminating spears of light, and so, no
longer drinking from the chalice of
suffering, I walk in search of buried
wings, as petals of a frozen heart spill
across a paper moon and
love,

love the most delicate flower of all,
finally blooms

DUSK
Looking Glass................9
Breathe..........................15
Black Rainbow 19
Bonfire...........................22
Ruby Tears....................26
Buttercup Sky 29

TWILIGHT
Whispers of Love 32
Fallen Petals......................35
Galaxy of Wonder 39
Crystallized.......................43
The Abyss..........................45
Oversized Emotions..........48
Love...................................52

DAWN
New Dawn........................56
Moonbeams 58
Serenity.............................60
Becoming..........................62
Stillness.............................65
Coming Home 68

DUSK

lay me down in the arms of love
until I find the light lost within

Looking Glass

through the looking glass
of my soul I wander,
trapped in corridors of
an insidious mind where
my heart, strings of pain kiss and
curdling thoughts wash through
veins in a trickling stream of
pain, where whispers of love
no longer breathe and
salacious dreams of freedom,
lit between shades of
a burning sun and a ravenous
moon, billow in clouds of flames,
as memories to dust fall and
blood orange rivers flood my skin,
smothering the sky

Love fell silently from my heart, petal by petal, until all that was left, were dried up tears watering pain. I was always good at supressing my emotions, afraid my truth would make others feel uncomfortable. Sexual assault, physically and mentally left scars with open wounds, stretched across the frontiers of my mind. Scars I decorated with smiles and the colours of happiness.

My relationship with intimacy, never did begin with love. It began with insecurity, a drunken night and a guy, whose name I don't remember. In a daydream of lust, I left the bar, hand in hand with a stranger, as the snow, pure and white fell upon my flushed cheeks.

That split moment, balancing between light and dark, was enough to make me feel wanted, enough to fulfil my low self-esteem and my longing to be anyone else, except the girl looking back in the mirror. That moment was enough to split my heart in two. Following my self-deprecating behaviour, physical intimacy never grew from a place of love. My exhausting need for men to find me attractive was glued to my heart in neediness. I began using sex as a tool, like one of my makeup brushes, fanning my pain, to make myself feel good. To feel good, until the light of the 'morning after', so cruelly brought nothing, but a harsh reality. But things were about to change, or so it seemed.

After graduating from University, I met a very charming older and wealthy man, to whom my insecurity wrapped around like a warm blanket. I cuddled into the illusion of love and the possibility of being happy. And I willingly trusted the promises made by my ego to my heart that this was the relationship that would mend the cracks. The one that would fix me. Yet, falling further into the arms of my ego, left me even more riddled with self-doubt and anxiety. My mind, harvesting negativity, left me standing yet again alone, wearing nothing but the cloths of pain and shame. I went from being someone this man was proud of, to something hanging off his arm, my glitter fading as the seasons passed and snow-capped love iced my breaking heart. On our final night together, after several rows, I awoke to the feeling of breathlessness and watched helplessly as love plucked the last petals from my wilting heart.

Today, I realise how this relationship was spun from a tornado of self-made and harmful emotions. How could I have found love for myself through the illusion of loving someone else? The pattern was toxic, soul destroying and destructive to whom I truly was. It was only when I woke up one morning, finally unable to smile in my own skin that my life was truly ready to change. I took responsibility for my actions, opened a new chapter in my life and decided to forgive myself. It was only then, that I began to realise that I was worth more than what my ego was telling me. To feel the warmth in my heart again, would mean a long journey ahead. But as I stood there that morning, when the sun seemed to shine a little brighter than usual, I looked the mirror in the eye.

And without flinching, I had to believe that I was not broken.

Breathe

between the lines of a blurred mind
emotions rise at high tide, swift
like air twirling beads of caution,
gathering speed through specks of
volcanic ash, dancing on shoulders and
spinning a pirouette of flames, until a
wall of ice melts smouldering words
and eyes align to see the aftermath of
what might have been, what might
have been if I had stopped to breathe

One breath, in, out. One breath can change everything. I was a big reactor growing up. Reacting to everything around me. And at times, I have to catch myself from falling into the same mindset, a familiar story riddled with lies. Through this overwhelming storm of insecurity, I reacted not to other people but to my own thoughts. It was exhausting and soul destroying at times.

    An early memory that continues to remind me of this, is from a shopping trip after school with my Mum. I was carrying one of those oversized schoolbags, a trend at the time, which I had to have to fit in. But of course, I never did fit in. There were two girls walking alongside us, chatting and giggling, making fun of me or so, I convinced myself. As we walked through the entrance door of a shopping centre, in a split moment of self-loathing and anger, feeling belittled and threatened, I purposely knocked one of the girls with my bag. What I didn't expect was for them to follow us around on our shopping trip before my Mum had to intervene. While this little snippet of my life, does provide some entertainment in my family, it highlights how deeply rooted my low self-esteem was.

    If I had felt at peace in myself, I certainly wouldn't have played into my egos greedy little game and let the dramatic narrative in my mind deflate my sense of self. Some of us grow up feeling confident and gifted with the fruits of self-belief. I on the other hand found myself torn between my parents working-class background and trying to fit in at a private school. I felt unsure of who I was and how I was meant to behave. I constantly felt that I had to prove my worth over and over again and it was exhausting.

In the years that followed, I continued to react to situations in my life, living through the monologue of my mind and giving into all the emotional triggers that were yet to heal. But I learned that by taking one conscious breath in and out, you can allow your mind a moment of stillness.

This exercise is not always easy, but you can change the entire decision and outcome of a situation by practicing it. And the more you practice it, the more it becomes a habit. In a storm that has no direction, I began to follow the winds of change.

Black Rainbow

twilight thoughts lie neatly packed
between dizzying cloths of velveteen
whispers and wrapped up dreams on
the brink of darkness,

a sour mind numbed with tears, holds
the lock on tomorrow's moon where
happiness, chewed up
is thrown to the bottom of a well
weeping,

rattling in a cage full of future demise,
the truth, a terror anchored at bay,
surfaces, and I, beneath the shadows of
a black rainbow
bathe in salted wounds

After ending the relationship with my long-term boyfriend, I buried my heart and ran across the world to the land of promised rainbows. Not in search of something wonderful but to escape everything that had held me a prisoner of my mind.

For a while, Australia sang all the promises and dreams that my heart, home on Irish soil could not hold onto. But it didn't take long for my life at the other side of the world to quickly mirror everything I was running away from. Not only that, my mental health deteriorated. I lost myself more and more in the negative landslide that were my thoughts. And I attracted everything unstable into my life, until there were more storms than rainbows.

Soon, chaos became my control drama. And home went from luxury to lying in a room of a shared house, crowded with 10 backpackers, half a roof missing and not being able to get out of my bed bug infested mattress. At that point, being bitten by bed bugs seemed someway cathartic of the pain that was destroying me from inside.

It took two years in Australia hating myself, to finally return home where my true journey was only about to begin. But not before everything that hurt my heart was unleashed and exorcised from my mind.

Bonfire

love kissed my feet,
a skip and a jump into my heart,
breathing hope in clouds of
faded glitter, coddling my
thoughts into believing
this world was mine to hug,
until strangled by a loose mind,
into the bonfire of my
soul I step, where sparkles of
temptation ignite ghosts of past and
in dreams of wax pain breathes
in the flickering shadows of
a burnt-out wick

Love, as delicate as a daisy, yet the only thing truly strong enough to heal us. In my quest for love, I looked beyond the horizon, throwing wishes to stars and dreaming on another moon. Never realising that what I truly desired was held in chains around my heart, begging to be freed. I only had to journey inside but too afraid of what the shadows would bring to light, I continued to patch up my wounds, using other people's words as my band aid.

My life was enriched with negativity. And still, I could not understand why I hadn't found 'the one'. I looked for him in all the same places I found myself lost in. And I constantly labelled lust as love. As a string of failed relationships spun like a web around my life, I danced like a puppet to the emotionally triggered thoughts in my head. I didn't know that I could change my thoughts, that my thoughts could change my actions. That my actions could lead me to heal.

But taking a knife to your pain and ripping it free makes you feel defensive about giving it all up. Afterall, I was fully committed to my pain. I wore it radiantly, wrapped around my mind, dressing my skin. It was my weapon of choice, my shield. If it meant that I had to now tell myself that I was wrong, that I was enough and worthy of receiving love, then I wasn't sure if I was ready to make that sacrifice.

Above all, I had spent all of those years investing in my book of pain. That's the irony of healing. It no longer requires using pain as a comfort blanket to justify your life. Even when pain is the only thing you feel comfortable wearing.

Ruby Tears

in the end, nothing was left
but the stem of an empty glass
stained with ruby tears,
tears, no longer hot
from fresh pricked eyes
but cold and dried up from drinking
too many times the same lie,
a lie that lay between the sheets
and kissed goodnight, a lie
that crept from the shadows
into my eyes,
a lie I swallowed too many times,
a lie, no longer mine

Truth and lies, falling like sand through time. A mirage of love and a disenchanted life weighed heavy on my soul. But as light peeped through the cracks of dusk, it was time to grieve the loss of who I imagined myself to be. Time to forgive myself. Self-deprecating thoughts are skilled in chipping away at our self-esteem and self-belief. And when you don't know how to heal pain, you wear it in armour. You wear it on every date you go on and lie in bed wearing it in every new relationship. I spent so much energy drinking up my own lies. I did everything except, make me better. Only I could be responsible for the recovery of my life.

    And while, we have no control over the past or the future, we can change how we think about ourselves in this single moment called the now. This present moment is all we ever truly experience.

Buttercup Sky

every night, the moon
from her garden of light, a
star plucks and into my mind
floats, teaspoons of dreams
sprinkling across my skin and
kissing my mind with
drops of dew as wishes
into thoughts breathe and
love beneath a buttercup sky
no longer sleeps, where stars
burning into snowflakes weep
and the cloaked face of night
cradles the break of day

Letting go of a myriad of toxic emotions was not easy. But the shackles of the past no longer felt comfortable and I craved something more than pain could provide. I craved freedom. The freedom to look myself in the mirror, to accept myself, to wear my skin with love. I began to understand that I had a choice. That I could believe what my ego had dedicated its daily work to or listen to the silent echoes of my soul, that I was worthy, I was enough.

Growing to realise that I didn't have to resonate with every thought that ran through my head, was a monumental life lesson. And so, I began to undress my heart under the light of the moon and shed my armour of pain.

TWILIGHT

*I wasn't ready to fly but for the first
time, in a long time, I could breathe*

Whispers of Love

in the stillness,
between the beat of my heart
and whispers of love, my soul
awakens from a casket of dreams,
rose petal scars spilling in light across
my skin, as thorns of pain from my
mind I pull and wounds
dipped in lavender skies I dress in
threads of scarlet jewels,
no longer buried in a burrow of lies,
dust of dawn slowly rises and I,
stung by tears wash clean my thoughts

We shed the layers of who we are, when they no longer serve to remind us of the lessons we need to learn. Pain once tarnished and then healed makes space for new beginnings. And while self-acceptance is not always easy, to love yourself first from the heart and not critique from the mind is key.

I had worn so many different versions of myself that to finally step into the truth of who I was, meant I had a little spring cleaning to do. Clearing the cobwebs from my heart included leaving behind many of my intimate relationships with male friends. Friends who had become in a way a safety net for my heart.

But the biggest transition I made that brought me closer to feeling peace, happened by allowing myself the freedom to be me. And to do this, I had to finally let go of my anger and forgive my younger and reckless self. The person who had treated my heart with disregard and disrespect. And I had to learn to do this without judgement.

Those lingering demons, nesting in sleeping wounds are not worth keeping, but they are important to acknowledge and heal. The ghosts of the past might feel real but only if you allow your mind to bury you there.

Fallen Petals

I was brand new, breath,
fresh like dawn of summer petals,
planting flutters of love through season
of heart, but in between the promises of
never letting my mind sleep, without a
kiss from my soul, the sun across my
skin set and

circle of darkness to land barren of
light drifted, where honey no longer
sweet, remembers to smile and love, a
whisper too late, no longer stirs, where
skin claws at splintered rock drowning,
under waves of bone poking and ripped
veins, where demons bleed behind
curtains of eyes and seeds of hope
rustle in silence

Relationships are a paradigm of mysteries but the one we have with ourselves can be the most heart-breaking of all. Who else can tell our heart so many lies that we unconsciously choose to believe? Becoming a Mum was one of the most beautiful blessings in my life. Yet, Motherhood resurrected all of those sleeping demons that my ego loved to nibble on. An old bully waiting patiently for me at the playground with snide remarks and a bag full of thoughts that chipped away at my identity and self-esteem. Was I good enough? Was I even enough?

Two years later, with two babies in nappies of different ages and I was left feeling completely overwhelmed. And scoop in living abroad, without the family network I grew up with supporting me and I was officially drowning under the weight of my mind. I became a shadow unrecognisable to myself. I lost my femininity and lust for feeling desired. This new Mum outfit I was wearing made me question, if all the things that had made me sparkle were now faded in burp cloths and milk stains?

    I had gone from working in a fast-paced industry, interviewing top hair celebs and travelling to international events, to wearing maternity leggings because I didn't know who I was dressing up as anymore. But it was the guilt of all of these feelings, more than anything else that hurt the most.

Sometimes, to regain our light we need to endure the darkness and embrace all the messy parts of us that need to heal.

And so, in the darkness between the stars and the moon, I began to accept life in all its chaos and beauty and fill my unwritten pages with words of love and healing. I kissed goodbye to my ego and hopped off the carousal.

Galaxy of Wonder

by the pull of strings,
notes of chords struck my
thoughts, picking and strumming,
until all I heard, were lyrics to a song
no longer mine,
but in sleep, my mind into pastures
green wanders, where dreams in
meadows of uncut stems graze and toes
into crystal waters dip,
where the breeze warm, tickles my skin
in melodies of Spring and beneath a
rose-lit moon dances with my heart,
and so, with eyes shining toward a
galaxy of wonder, no longer tangled in
a web of stars, I kiss the dawn of a new
horizon and love, a vessel of hope
guides me home

To dream, is to hold a sprinkle of magic at our fingertips. So often we neglect the colourful side of our mind where we allow our imagination to run wild and free. And so often growing up, we've been told that our dreams are unrealistic, impossible and to get our heads out of the clouds. And at some point, we start to believe that.

    When I was younger, I wanted to be an Astronaut because I wanted to fly amongst the stars. Today, I'm not launching into Space, but I do get to write beneath the twinkling sky. This bridge between childhood dreams and adulthood is often broken, by simply not replacing old dreams with new ones. Not caring for our mind and all the possibility that lives within, is neglecting our mental health and this easily manifests in low self-esteem, self-loathing and everything that goes against our natural state. Self-care is not only about looking after ourselves physically but also taking steps to care for our mind and emotions.

Writing has always been my chosen therapy. Bleeding pain and heartache, love, and joy across the pages of my journal. Yet after the birth of my second son, I stopped writing. I woke up one day and never picked up my pen. It was easier to hide behind my fear than to face my emotions on paper. But those unsung words took their toll until the emotions, like a riptide of pain, spun out of control and spilled in tears of ink from my heart.

Finally, I could begin to breathe again. Whatever dreams linger in your heart, allow them to feel the light and

to be your magnet through whatever
darkness comes your way.

Crystallized

in fires of darkness,
a sniper of thoughts
roast along the bones of my
mind, yet my skin
wrapped in challis cloths of
love, steals into shadows of a
promised land, where love broken, in
second chances glisten and the
chrysalis of my thoughts into colours of
sunrise split, where the echo of
hummingbirds in tumbling milkweeds
sing and the past crystallized
into love shines, the flame of fear
doused by the warrior of light burning
within

As interrogating thoughts hustle your mind, igniting anxiety and feeding self-criticism, imagine how differently it would feel to live without your mind steering the way. One of my favourite quotes is by the renowned Jim Rohn, 'If you don't like how things are done, change it! You're not a tree.' And so, if we don't like how our story is looking, we have the choice not to rewrite our past but to write from blank pages of a new beginning.

So many of our negative and doubting emotions are triggered by pain and its sidekick fear. But when we allow our thoughts to pause, our mind has the opportunity to be responsive. Without fear hovering around in our mind, we have an open space to embrace the freedom of who we are.

The Abyss

daylight undresses as the moon, in
restless thoughts, conceals her light,
cotton blankets bury eyes sleeping in
tired lines of a cherry smile, dancing
with tears turned to water drowning
yet, through the mist of growing
darkness, my feet into the abyss of love
dive and no longer breathing a life I
once chose to wear, I swim ashore

Between the constellations of light and dark, love in all its audaciousness and chaos found me. While I had allowed pain to feed on my body, I decided that I had enough of the constant hangover from my mind. I had allowed the past to be my resting place for all of my wounds and by doing so my heart had taken up camp there. And so, no longer feeling overwhelmed by the pain that was streaming through my thoughts, I let go.

Healing open wounds takes time but deciding to let go of the hurt is the beginning of a new life. On days when the clouds hug the land and life feels uncertain, I no longer take flight into the darkness, diving into my old habits and snuggling into my scars, I fight back. On these days, it is important to embrace the things that give us joy, even if it is as simple as taking a bath or going for a walk. It's okay, to not always be okay, but by letting go, the clouds will rain and with it our fears and anxieties wash away. Rainbows breathe in between storms and cloudless skies.

Oversized Emotions

can you hear me? rapturous
mind devouring this cyclonic
silence of emotions, stitched
illusions of pain and pockets filled with
cheque books and tear stained notes
I've cashed into a bank of memories,
crinkled with scars, impaling the pages
of my eyes,

I have worn this weight too long,
this breath too heavy with the
stench of loves death, where the air
dusted with petals is ripped from
wings cut up and buried but
I hold on, shedding my coat
from a Winter born in Spring and
under a sea of stars ask the
moon not yet to sleep, as
trepidation kisses strings of light

and love unveils, warming the
pallor of a distant moon

My heart has always beat to the lyrics of my emotions, messy and oversized. As an empath, it has been important for me to learn how to differentiate between my own feelings and those of others, which dust off easily on my mind. Sometimes these borrowed emotions have triggered old feelings and I would become unhappy or feel drained without apparent reason. This meant my emotions were always being delicately held in the balance of how other people were feeling. But I learned to become aware and by disrupting this conditioned monologue, I was able to take control of my emotional wellbeing.

By bringing our thoughts into the present moment, we can calm our mind. It feels strange yet empowering to gain an awareness of what you are feeling and of the emotions that so often dress our skin unexpectedly.

Love

love felt too pure for my lips,
until the rain came and washed
darkness into streams of light,
where fear from my mind spills,
evanescing into ravines of my heart
breathing forgiveness into
all the places I could
no longer reach,
love felt too pure for my lips
until stars made from snowdust
kissed the sun and in the
arms of darkness, I finally
found the guiding light

The power of love was no longer silent, as the tears from my heart spilt freely from my eyes and the scars from my mouth began to heal. And I said the words I was always too afraid to hear, 'I forgive myself'. Although it might feel impossible to forgive those who have born hurt into our hearts, by holding onto pain, it manifests as anger, toxic and harmful.

    Despite the painful process of healing, I slowly began to look in the mirror that had for so many years shattered my self-esteem and smile back from my heart. It is important to remember that blame, even if it is justified or not, is another form of self-harm. It diverts our attention away from what matters, to heal. Forgiveness is not about denying it to someone we blame, it is about allowing ourselves to feel peace. This realisation didn't come easy but as I fell beneath the reflection of the glassy lake that offered an escape for a fleeting moment to the pain that consumed my thoughts, I had a choice. And from that day on, I made the choice to fight back.

DAWN

clouds rain letting go,
I cry, finally letting you in

New Dawn

winter leaves rustle beneath a
stormy sea, until I remember,
there are days when I look at the sky
and all of my thoughts are dazzled
by colours born from a kiss,
a kiss ferried on wings, drifting
between the rain and the clouds,
where pearly droplets sprinkle love,
watering the land and cradling
waves of hope and so,
into the eyes of a new dawn I dive,
light no longer seeping into whispers of
darkness but breathing in all the
colours I dare to dream

I was awakening to the possibility of allowing love to rush through my veins and wrap my skin in rays of warmth. And yet, there were so many times when darkness crept through my mind. As human beings we are composed of both light and dark, the moon, and the sun. And so, we shouldn't try to bypass our darkness. Instead, we must embrace it without fear and learn how to heal it. We must dig deep into the soil and pull out the roots of our pain.

    The garden of our soul needs to be continuously watered for new possibilities to blossom and flourish. Even when our mind is heavy with self-doubt, luring us across rocky tides, we must choose to swim against the current. We must fight to breathe the light inside.

Moonbeams

lace my skin with threads of love
and through hazel skies paint
flickers of light, in
glittering cheeks of moonbeam
tears dress my lips with
drops of sunshine and on petals of
sanguine eyes let streams of serenity
flow across traces of lemon skin, where
thoughts into sand no longer fall and I,
a firefly born from the soul of night
soar beyond the horizon of my mind

Our skin is the tapestry of our hearts stories and our heartbeat the frequency of our soul. When I began to look at myself through eyes of love, to allow myself to be transparent and vulnerable, I opened up my heart. Love is the single most powerful cure for all of our pain, and we have unlimited access from within ourselves.

The exhilaration I felt, when I no longer depended on anyone else to fulfil my desire for love was something I had never before experienced. To allow myself to feel that freedom was the most beautiful and empowering emotion I could have ever wished for. It has made me a better Mum and a better person. To trust in yourself with love and without hesitation is the single most beautiful gift you can give to yourself.

Serenity

I rise beyond the stream of thought
that hugs the air in lingering fear, I
breathe through rivers of paper moons
and creep through tunnels of lacuna,
yet lips skim dotted lies undressing
in melancholy sighs, and my mind
awakens to skies feeling blue
but serenity dipped in lashes of tears
wraps warm my heart and under
the pallid light of the moon, in
flickering shadows of a flaxen sun, I
watch as light and dark coalesce into
flames of a kiss,
loves enigma unveiled between
the land and the sky

I have always struggled with balancing the opposing sides of my mind. On the one hand, my thoughts are fuelling me with confidence until they collide with the demons restless, waiting to upsurge peace.

But I have learned to overcome my fear of feeling the darkness. By letting it flow through my mind, I can also exhale it from my thoughts. I can feel it, but I am not consumed by it. And I no longer believe all that my mind has been willing to sell.

We exist in the dualities of light and dark and breathe in all the shades of colour, which we allow our mind to embrace.

Becoming

the road is quiet,
empty of rushing by thoughts,
hollers and honks of minds jetting
to tomorrow on yesterday's moon,
the land is sleeping, yet dreams
hibernating in wandering stars, stir a
breath as light, struggling to climb
mountain tops rise beyond the sky and
a labyrinth of disarray unravels into
meandering thoughts,
where I swap crosses for stars and
night, through heliophile eyes hug
flowers of the sun, where murky
pillows unveil the dawning of moon
and light traces my heart in shadows of
wings ready to take flight,
where the wind and I embrace dancing
along the horizon of a new life

The greatest loss we can experience in life, is to see all the missing pieces of a puzzle from another person's story because we do not know how to write our own. When I didn't trust the path, my soul was to journey, I listened to everyone else's advice, except that from my own heart. I searched for outward approval, instead of looking inward. I ignored the bones of love that were rattling with answers and I drowned the light inside with fear.

We may not always be ready to listen and hear the truth speak but when we allow ourselves the freedom to explore our life, we discover that we are capable of great things. When I tore down all of the walls that had been suffocating my skin and pulled off the masks that were not mine, it felt like I was seeing my life for the first time. It felt like I was waking up. I had been lost for so long and finally, I was coming home. Coming home to the light within, means you will never remain a prisoner of your mind.

Stillness

From chapped lips of oblivion, I dive
swimming through valleys
and bathing in the vanilla whisper
of fireflies and dragonflies,
fear sinking beneath the rubble of
debris, as the last cloud of pain drifts
through crevasses no longer anchored
by blue speckled thoughts and
rainbows undressed in the silhouette of
night, where petals of the sun into the
arms of my soul leap and I, ready to
sail across open seas listen to the lull of
waves humming in the stillness of love,
this, my final journey through a
kaleidoscope of stars, illuminates
in the kiss between my
heart and my mind

I found stillness, a fleeting moment but I learned of its existence, magical in its essence. A space between the noise, a breath between the chaos. It swam through rivers of my soul bringing peace to my mind and love to my heart. No longer a servant to my thoughts but an observer, I began to realise that life is never without stormy waters but finding moments of inner peace helps to soothe a bustling mind.

By being aware of the present moment it puts a stop to the running monologue between our ears. And when we accept that where we are in life, is where we need to be right now, we are no longer resisting important messages and lessons to learn. And when we learn those lessons, we shed the weight of our pain. No longer stitched to the past but free to evolve

beyond the limits of our resistance.
Stepping into my truth was the real
beginning of my journey home.

Coming Home

the ocean light casts a shadow of doubt,
fear growing and darkening the way
but this my longest journey, under
threat by egos mind cannot be left to
steal away, lungs filled with the taste of
freedom, as the air soft and hazy tickles
my skin, where grains of hope dance
between my toes and I, no longer lost
beneath a cloud of waves dress in rays
of translucency,
the tide calms and in bubbles of
light I breathe, as a crystal orbit of
stars, born in darkness, open in eyes
shut, feet step ashore and finally,
tasting the salted air of my soul, I look
to the moon and smile, I am home

Our journey is never complete, the battle never fought and won. As parts of life heal, it is important to remember that healing continues in every breath of light you breathe. On days when colours feel faded, when the sky hurts your eyes or the rain feels like fire burning your skin, take a moment to think about what you can feel grateful for.

    Gratitude is not just a word but a feeling that resonates within your heart. I like to write down some of the things that happen in my day or week that bring me a heartfelt feeling of joy and pop them into a gratitude jar. They can be as small as a cup of coffee from my husband or as big as achieving one of my goals. This jar becomes like a treasure pot filled with moments you can look back on and ignite this feeling of gratitude into your life. So, on those days, when you are wrapped in blankets of clouds, read one of these notes. Believe in that moment of joy, that it existed and that it will exist again.

Our mind is the paintbrush in this great masterpiece we create called life. And even though the tides between our ego and our heart might sail across turbulent waters, we can work to create harmony between them both. I believe that while our mind might not always support our heart, together they create the soul of who we are.

To my beautiful readers, thank you for sharing this journey from dusk into dawn. Blessings of love and healing in your life.

From your author,

-Natasha.

Follow Natasha on social media:

Instagram @daysloves

PAPER MOON

Copyright © Natasha Tynan 2020

Illustrator & cover design Martina Francone 2020

All rights reserved. This book or any portion thereof may not be reproduced or used in any manner whatsoever without the express written permission of the publisher except for the use of brief quotations in a book review.

Printed by Kindle direct publishing.

ISBN: 9798666047477

First printing, 2020.